I0446462

The Art of Influence

The Art of Influence:

How to Persuade, Negotiate and Inspire Others

RIKROSES BOOKS AND E-BOOKS

SUMMARY

INTRODUCTION: Why Influence Matters

Influence is the ability to change the behavior, beliefs or actions of others in a positive and ethical way. Influence is not manipulation, coercion or deception. Influence is not something you have or don't have. Influence is something you can learn, develop and master.

In this book, you will discover the science and the art of influence. You will learn the psychological principles that underlie human behavior and decision-making. You will explore the practical techniques that can help you persuade, negotiate and inspire others in any situation. You will also learn how to avoid the common pitfalls and challenges that can hinder your influence.

This book is divided into four parts. The first part covers the foundations of influence, including why influence matters, how it works and what makes it effective. The second part introduces the 12 principles of influence, which are based on decades of research and evidence from psychology, neuroscience and behavioral economics. The third part focuses on the skills and strategies of influence, such as storytelling, framing, questioning, listening, mirroring, reciprocity, scarcity, authority, social proof, liking, commitment and consistency and contrast. The fourth part deals with the applications and implications of influence, such as negotiation, resistance, ethics and practice.

By reading this book, you will gain a deeper understanding of yourself and others. You will be able to communicate more effectively, persuasively and confidently. You will be able to achieve your goals and create positive outcomes for yourself and others. You will be able to become a master influencer.

5

CHAPTER 1: The Psychology of Influence

What is influence and why does it matter? Influence is the ability to change or affect someone's behavior, thoughts, feelings, or decisions. Influence is not manipulation, coercion, or deception. Influence is not about forcing someone to do something they don't want to do. Influence is about helping someone to see things from a different perspective, to understand the benefits of a certain action, to overcome their doubts or fears, or to align their values with yours.

Influence matters because it is essential for success in any field or endeavor. Whether you are a leader, a manager, a salesperson, a teacher, a parent, a friend, or a partner, you need influence to achieve your goals and to make a positive impact on others. Influence can help you to persuade others to support your ideas, to negotiate better deals, to inspire others to follow your vision, to resolve conflicts, to build trust and rapport, to motivate others to perform better, and to create lasting change.

But how does influence work? What are the psychological factors that affect how people respond to your attempts to influence them? How can you use these factors to increase your influence and improve your outcomes? In this chapter, we will explore the psychology of influence and learn how to apply it in various situations. We will cover the following topics:

- **The four types of influence:** rational, emotional, social, and personal
- **The six stages of influence:** attention, interest, desire, action, satisfaction, and loyalty
- **The three levels of influence:** compliance, identification, and internalization

6

- The four sources of influence: credibility, logic, emotion, and relationship
- The four styles of influence: assertive, cooperative, passive, and aggressive
- The four barriers to influence: lack of trust, lack of interest, lack of understanding, and lack of agreement

The four types of influence: rational, emotional, social, and personal.

Rational influence is based on facts, logic, and evidence. It appeals to the reason and intellect of the audience. Emotional influence is based on feelings, values, and beliefs. It appeals to the emotions and motivations of the audience. Social influence is based on norms, expectations, and conformity. It appeals to the need for belonging and acceptance of the audience. Personal influence is based on identity, character, and charisma. It appeals to the self-image and aspirations of the audience.

The six stages of influence: attention, interest, desire, action, satisfaction, and loyalty.

Attention is the first stage of influence, where you capture the attention of the audience and make them aware of your message. Interest is the second stage of influence, where you arouse the interest of the audience and make them curious about your message. Desire is the third stage of influence, where you create the desire of the audience and make them want your message. Action is the fourth stage of influence, where you persuade the audience to take action and make them do your message. Satisfaction is the fifth stage of influence, where you satisfy the audience and make them happy with your message. Loyalty is the sixth stage of influence, where you retain the audience and make them loyal to your message.

The three levels of influence: compliance, identification, and internalization.

Compliance is the lowest level of influence, where the audience agrees with your message because of external rewards or punishments. Identification is the middle level of influence, where the audience agrees with your message because of social or personal identification with you. Internalization is the highest level of influence, where the audience agrees with your message because of internal values or beliefs.

The four sources of influence: credibility, logic, emotion, and relationship.

7

Credibility is the source of influence that comes from your expertise, reputation, and trustworthiness. Logic is the source of influence that comes from your arguments, evidence, and reasoning. Emotion is the source of influence that comes from your feelings, stories, and images. Relationship is the source of influence that comes from your rapport, empathy, and connection.

The four styles of influence: assertive, cooperative, passive, and aggressive.

Assertive style is the style of influence that expresses your message clearly and confidently without violating the rights or feelings of others. Cooperative style is the style of influence that expresses your message respectfully and collaboratively while seeking mutual benefits or solutions. Passive style is the style of influence that expresses your message weakly or indirectly while avoiding conflict or confrontation. Aggressive style is the style of influence that expresses your message forcefully or rudely while violating the rights or feelings of others.

The four barriers to influence: lack of trust, lack of interest, lack of understanding, and lack of agreement.

- Lack of trust is the barrier to influence that occurs when the audience does not trust you or your message.
- Lack of interest is the barrier to influence that occurs when the audience does not care about you or your message.
- Lack of understanding is the barrier to influence that occurs when the audience does not understand you or your message.
- Lack of agreement is the barrier to influence that occurs when the audience does not agree with you or your message.

By understanding the psychology of influence, you will be able to tailor your approach and strategy to suit different people and situations. You will be able to communicate more effectively and persuasively. You will be able to overcome resistance and objections. You will be able to create win-win outcomes and long-term relationships. You will be able to become a more influential person.

8

CHAPTER 2: The Principles of Influence

Influence is the ability to change someone's mind, behavior, or decision in a way that benefits you or your cause. Influence is not manipulation, coercion, or deception. Influence is based on trust, respect, and mutual understanding. Influence is a skill that can be learned and improved with practice.

But how do you influence others effectively? What are the secrets of persuasive communication? What are the factors that make people say yes to your requests?

In this chapter, we will explore the six universal principles of influence that have been identified by Dr. Robert Cialdini, a renowned social psychologist and author of the best-selling book Influence: The Psychology of Persuasion. These principles are:

- **Reciprocity:** People tend to return favors and feel obligated to repay debts.
- **Scarcity:** People value things more when they are rare or limited.
- **Authority:** People tend to follow the advice or commands of experts or credible sources.
- **Social proof:** People tend to look at what others are doing or thinking before making their own decisions.
- **Liking:** People tend to agree with or help those they like or find attractive.
- **Commitment and consistency:** People tend to stick to their previous choices or actions and seek consistency in their beliefs and behaviors.

Reciprocity

9

This principle states that people tend to return favors and feel obligated to repay debts. When someone does something nice for you, you feel a sense of gratitude and a desire to reciprocate. You can use this principle to increase your chances of getting a positive response from someone by offering them something valuable or helpful first, such as a compliment, a gift, a favor, or a concession. By doing so, you create a feeling of indebtedness in the other person, which makes them more likely to agree to your request or offer.

Scarcity

This principle states that people value things more when they are rare or limited. When something is scarce, it seems more attractive, desirable, and valuable. You can use this principle to increase the perceived value of your product, service, idea, or proposal by highlighting its uniqueness, exclusivity, or urgency. For example, you can emphasize how your offer is different from others, how it is only available for a limited time or quantity, or how it will solve a pressing problem or need.

Authority

This principle states that people tend to follow the advice or commands of experts or credible sources. When someone is seen as an authority, they have more influence and power over others. You can use this principle to enhance your credibility and trustworthiness by demonstrating your expertise, experience, qualifications, or achievements. For example, you can cite relevant facts, statistics, testimonials, endorsements, or credentials to support your claims or recommendations.

Social proof

This principle states that people tend to look at what others are doing or thinking before making their own decisions. When someone is unsure about something, they rely on the opinions or actions of others to guide them. You can use this principle to influence others by showing them that many people like them have already done what you want them to do, or agree with what you want them to think. For example, you can use social media reviews, ratings, comments, likes, shares, or followers to show the popularity or approval of your offer.

Liking

This principle states that people tend to agree with or help those they like or find attractive. When someone likes you, they are more willing to listen to you,

10

cooperate with you, and comply with your requests. You can use this principle to increase your likability and rapport with others by showing genuine interest in them, finding common ground with them, giving them sincere compliments, using humor and positive emotions, and mirroring their body language and tone of voice.

Commitment and consistency

This principle states that people tend to stick to their previous choices or actions and seek consistency in their beliefs and behaviors. When someone makes a commitment, they feel a psychological pressure to act in ways that are consistent with it. You can use this principle to influence others by getting them to make small commitments first, and then gradually increasing the level of commitment until they reach your desired outcome. For example, you can ask for a small favor, a simple opinion, a sign-up, a trial, or a low-cost purchase first, and then follow up with a bigger request or offer later.

These principles are based on decades of scientific research and experiments that show how human beings respond to various social situations and stimuli. They are not mere tricks or techniques, but fundamental aspects of human psychology that can be used for good or evil purposes.

Understanding these principles will help you become a more effective influencer, whether you want to persuade your boss, your customers, your colleagues, your friends, or your family. You will learn how to apply these principles in different contexts and scenarios, and how to avoid being influenced by others who may use them against you.

By mastering these principles, you will be able to create win-win outcomes for yourself and others, and achieve your personal and professional goals with greater ease and success.

CHAPTER 3: The Power of Storytelling

One of the most effective ways to influence others is to tell them a story. A story can capture their attention, engage their emotions, and persuade them to take action. But what makes a good story? And how can you use storytelling to enhance your influence?

In this chapter, we will explore the power of storytelling and how it can help you achieve your goals. We will learn:

- Why stories are so influential and how they work on the human brain
- How to craft a compelling story that resonates with your audience
- How to use different types of stories for different purposes and contexts
- How to avoid common storytelling mistakes and pitfalls
- How to apply storytelling techniques to your own situations and challenges

By the end of this chapter, you will have a better understanding of the art and science of storytelling and how to use it to your advantage.

Why stories are so influential and how they work on the human brain

Stories are everywhere. We read them in books, watch them on TV, listen to them on podcasts, and tell them to each other. Stories are not just a form of entertainment, they are also a powerful way of communicating information, values, emotions, and experiences. Stories shape our understanding of ourselves, others, and the world around us. But why are stories so influential, and how do they work on the human brain?

12

One reason why stories are influential is that they capture and hold our attention. The human brain is constantly bombarded with sensory stimuli, but it cannot process everything at once. Therefore, it has to filter out what is irrelevant and focus on what is important. Stories provide a structure that helps the brain organize and prioritize information. They have a beginning, a middle, and an end, and they follow a predictable pattern of events that create suspense, curiosity, and interest. Stories also use vivid details, imagery, dialogue, and emotions that appeal to our senses and imagination. By engaging multiple cognitive processes, stories make us pay attention and remember what we hear or see.

Another reason why stories are influential is that they transport us into the characters' world. When we listen to or watch a story, we do not just observe it from a distance, we immerse ourselves in it. We create mental simulations of the story events and empathize with the characters. We feel what they feel, think what they think, and want what they want. This process is called narrative transportation, and it has several effects on our brain and behavior. First, it reduces our awareness of our surroundings and our self-consciousness, making us more open and receptive to the story message. Second, it increases our emotional involvement and identification with the characters, making us more likely to adopt their perspectives and values. Third, it enhances our memory and learning of the story content, making us more likely to recall and apply it later.

A third reason why stories are influential is that they trigger neurochemical changes in our brain that influence our mood, motivation, and social behavior. For example, stories that involve emotional arousal, such as fear, joy, or sadness, stimulate the release of cortisol and oxytocin in our brain. Cortisol is a hormone that increases our alertness and stress response, while oxytocin is a hormone that increases our trust and empathy. Together, these hormones make us more attentive to the story events and more connected to the characters. Another example is stories that involve moral dilemmas or heroic actions that stimulate the release of dopamine in our brain. Dopamine is a neurotransmitter that regulates our reward system and motivates us to pursue our goals. When we see someone overcome a challenge or achieve a positive outcome in a story, we feel a sense of satisfaction and inspiration that drives us to emulate their behavior or seek similar experiences.

In summary, stories are influential because they work on multiple levels of our brain: they capture our attention, transport us into another reality, and trigger neurochemical changes that affect our emotions, cognition, and actions. Stories are not just passive entertainment; they are active agents of change that can shape our beliefs, attitudes, values, and behaviors. Stories can make us laugh or cry; they can

13

make us think or feel; they can make us learn or act. Stories are powerful tools for communication that can influence individuals and societies in profound ways.

How to craft a compelling story that resonates with your audience

Storytelling is one of the most powerful ways to connect with your audience, convey your message, and inspire action. But how do you craft a compelling story that resonates with your audience? Here are some tips to help you create a captivating narrative that engages your listeners and moves them to action.

1) **Know your purpose.** Before you start writing your story, you need to have a clear idea of what you want to achieve with it. What is the main point you want to make? What is the emotion you want to evoke? What is the action you want to inspire? Having a clear purpose will help you shape your story and keep it focused and relevant.

2) **Know your audience.** The next step is to understand who you are writing for. Who are they? What are their needs, interests, challenges, and goals? What are their values, beliefs, and emotions? How do they communicate and consume information? Knowing your audience will help you tailor your story to their preferences and expectations.

3) **Choose a structure.** A good story has a beginning, a middle, and an end. The beginning sets the scene, introduces the characters, and hooks the audience's attention. The middle develops the plot, builds tension, and creates conflict. The end resolves the conflict, delivers the message, and calls for action. You can use different structures to organize your story, such as the hero's journey, the three-act structure, or the problem-solution-benefit framework.

4) **Use sensory details.** One of the best ways to make your story come alive is to use sensory details that appeal to the five senses: sight, sound, smell, taste, and touch. Sensory details help you create vivid images in your audience's mind, evoke emotions, and immerse them in your story world. For example, instead of saying "She was nervous", you can say "She felt her palms sweat and her heart race".

5) **Show, don't tell.** Another way to make your story more engaging is to show, not tell. This means using dialogue, action, and description to reveal your characters' personality, emotions, and motivations, rather than stating them directly. Showing allows your audience to infer and interpret your

14

story, rather than being told what to think or feel. For example, instead of saying "He was angry", you can say "He slammed his fist on the table".

6) **Use conflict and tension.** Conflict is the engine of any story. It creates drama, suspense, and interest. Conflict can be external (between characters or forces) or internal (within a character's mind or heart). You need to create conflict in your story to challenge your characters, test their values, and push them to change. Tension is the result of conflict. It keeps your audience on edge, wondering what will happen next and how the characters will overcome their obstacles.

7) **Have a clear message.** Your story should have a clear message that summarizes your main point and conveys your purpose. Your message should be relevant to your audience and aligned with their values and goals. Your message should also be memorable and actionable. You can use techniques such as repetition, rhyme, metaphor, or analogy to make your message stick in your audience's mind.

8) **End with a call to action.** The final step of crafting a compelling story is to end with a call to action that invites your audience to take the next step or apply what they learned from your story. Your call to action should be specific, clear, and urgent. You can use words such as "now", "today", or "join" to create a sense of immediacy and urgency.

By following these tips, you can craft a compelling story that resonates with your audience and inspires them to take action.

How to use different types of stories for different purposes and contexts

Stories are powerful tools for communication, persuasion and influence. They can capture attention, evoke emotions, convey messages and inspire action. But not all stories are created equal. Depending on the purpose and context of your communication, you need to choose the right type of story to achieve your desired outcome.

In this article, we will explore four types of stories that you can use for different purposes and contexts: anecdotal, factual, visionary and metaphorical. We will also provide some tips and examples on how to craft and deliver these stories effectively.

Anecdotal stories

15

Anecdotal stories are personal stories that illustrate a point or a lesson. They are often used to establish rapport, credibility and trust with your audience. They can also make abstract concepts more concrete and relatable.

Anecdotal stories are suitable for situations where you want to:

- Share your experience or expertise on a topic
- Connect with your audience on an emotional level
- Provide evidence or support for your argument or claim
- Inspire or motivate your audience to take action

To create an anecdotal story, you need to:

- Identify the main message or lesson that you want to convey
- Choose a relevant and memorable personal experience that illustrates your message or lesson
- Structure your story using the classic narrative arc: exposition, rising action, climax, falling action and resolution
- Use vivid details, sensory language and dialogue to make your story engaging and realistic
- Highlight the key takeaway or call to action at the end of your story

For example, if you want to persuade your audience to adopt a healthy lifestyle, you can share an anecdotal story about how you overcame a health challenge by changing your habits and mindset.

Factual stories

Factual stories are stories that present facts, data or information in a compelling way. They are often used to educate, inform or persuade your audience. They can also help you establish authority, credibility and trust on a topic.

Factual stories are suitable for situations where you want to:

- Explain a complex or technical topic in a simple and clear way
- Provide evidence or support for your argument or claim
- Compare and contrast different options or alternatives
- Highlight the benefits or consequences of a decision or action

16

To create a factual story, you need to:

- Identify the main message or point that you want to convey
- Choose relevant and reliable facts, data or information that support your message or point
- Structure your story using the classic narrative arc: exposition, rising action, climax, falling action and resolution
- Use visual aids, charts, graphs or diagrams to illustrate your facts, data or information
- Emphasize the key takeaway or call to action at the end of your story

For example, if you want to explain how climate change affects the environment and human health, you can use factual stories that show the causes, effects and solutions of climate change using scientific data and statistics.

Visionary stories

Visionary stories are stories that paint a picture of a desired future state or outcome. They are often used to inspire, motivate or persuade your audience. They can also help you create a shared vision, mission or goal with your audience.

Visionary stories are suitable for situations where you want to:

- Communicate your vision, mission or goal for yourself, your team or your organization
- Inspire or motivate your audience to join you in pursuing your vision, mission or goal
- Persuade your audience to adopt a new idea, perspective or behavior
- Challenge the status quo or overcome resistance to change

To create a visionary story, you need to:

- Identify the main message or point that you want to convey
- Choose a relevant and realistic future state or outcome that illustrates your message or point
- Structure your story using the classic narrative arc: exposition, rising action, climax, falling action and resolution

17

- Use vivid details, sensory language and imagery to make your story appealing and persuasive
- Highlight the key takeaway or call to action at the end of your story

For example, if you want to communicate your vision for a more sustainable and inclusive world, you can use visionary stories that show how people's lives would be improved by adopting green practices and embracing diversity.

Metaphorical stories

Metaphorical stories are stories that use metaphors, analogies or symbols to convey a message or a lesson. They are often used to simplify, clarify or amplify a complex or abstract concept. They can also help you create emotional resonance, interest and curiosity with your audience.

Metaphorical stories are suitable for situations where you want to:

- Simplify or clarify a complex or abstract concept
- Amplify or emphasize a message or a lesson
- Create emotional resonance, interest or curiosity with your audience
- Stimulate creativity or innovation with your audience

To create a metaphorical story, you need to:

- Identify the main message or lesson that you want to convey
- Choose a relevant and appropriate metaphor, analogy or symbol that represents your message or lesson
- Structure your story using the classic narrative arc: exposition, rising action, climax, falling action and resolution
- Use vivid details, sensory language and imagery to make your story engaging and meaningful
- Highlight the key takeaway or call to action at the end of your story

For example, if you want to simplify or clarify the concept of leadership, you can use metaphorical stories that compare leadership to different animals, such as lions, eagles or dolphins.

Conclusion

18

Stories are powerful tools for communication, persuasion and influence. By choosing the right type of story for your purpose and context, you can create a lasting impact on your audience. Remember to use the classic narrative arc, vivid details, sensory language and imagery to make your stories engaging and effective. And don't forget to highlight the key takeaway or call to action at the end of your stories. Happy storytelling!

How to avoid common storytelling mistakes and pitfalls

Storytelling is a powerful tool for influencing others, whether you are a leader, a marketer, a teacher, or a friend. Stories can capture attention, evoke emotions, inspire action, and persuade people to change their minds or behaviors. However, not all stories are equally effective. Some stories may fall flat, bore the audience, or even backfire. To avoid these common storytelling mistakes and pitfalls, here are some tips to follow:

- **Know your audience.** Before you craft your story, you need to understand who you are telling it to. What are their interests, needs, values, and goals? What are their pain points, challenges, and objections? How can your story address these aspects and resonate with them? Tailor your story to fit your audience and their context.

- **Have a clear purpose.** Why are you telling this story? What do you want to achieve with it? What is the main message or takeaway you want to convey? Having a clear purpose will help you structure your story and focus on the most relevant and impactful details. It will also help you measure the effectiveness of your story and adjust it if needed.

- **Use the classic story arc.** A good story has a beginning, a middle, and an end. It also has a protagonist, a conflict, and a resolution. The classic story arc follows this pattern: exposition (setting the scene and introducing the characters), rising action (building up the tension and the stakes), climax (reaching the peak of the conflict and the turning point), falling action (showing the consequences and the aftermath), and resolution (wrapping up the story and delivering the message). Following this arc will help you create a coherent and engaging story that keeps the audience hooked.

- **Show, don't tell.** One of the most common storytelling mistakes is telling the audience what to think or feel instead of showing them through vivid details, sensory descriptions, dialogue, actions, and emotions. Showing

19

allows the audience to experience the story for themselves and form their own impressions and connections. It also makes the story more memorable and persuasive. For example, instead of saying "She was scared", you can show her fear by saying "She felt her heart pounding in her chest, her palms sweating, her breath quickening".

- **Be authentic.** Another common storytelling pitfall is being dishonest or exaggerating the facts to make the story more dramatic or appealing. While some embellishment may be acceptable for creative purposes, lying or distorting the truth can damage your credibility and trustworthiness as a storyteller. The audience may feel betrayed or manipulated if they discover that your story is not based on reality. Therefore, be authentic and truthful when telling your story. If you need to change some details for privacy or clarity reasons, make sure to disclose that upfront.

- **Keep it simple.** A good story is not necessarily a long or complex one. In fact, simplicity can often enhance the effectiveness of your story by making it easier to understand and remember. Avoid unnecessary details, jargon, or technical terms that may confuse or distract the audience. Use simple language, short sentences, and clear transitions. Focus on the core elements of your story and eliminate anything that does not serve your purpose or message.

- **Practice and refine.** Finally, one of the best ways to avoid storytelling mistakes and pitfalls is to practice and refine your story before you share it with others. Practice telling your story out loud or writing it down. Get feedback from others who can offer constructive criticism and suggestions. Revise your story based on the feedback and your own observations. Repeat this process until you are confident and satisfied with your story.

How to apply storytelling techniques to your own situations and challenges

Storytelling is an art and a skill that can be learned and improved with practice and guidance. By following these tips, you can avoid common storytelling mistakes and pitfalls and create stories that influence others in positive ways.

Storytelling is a powerful tool for influencing others, whether you want to persuade, motivate, inspire, or educate. Stories can capture attention, create emotional connection, and make complex ideas more memorable and relatable.

20

But how can you apply storytelling techniques to your own situations and challenges? Here are some steps to help you craft and deliver effective stories.

1) **Identify your goal and audience.** Before you start writing your story, you need to have a clear idea of what you want to achieve and who you are speaking to. What is the main message or takeaway you want to convey? What action do you want your audience to take after hearing your story? How much do they know about the topic and what are their interests, needs, and concerns?

2) **Choose a relevant and relatable story.** Once you have your goal and audience in mind, you need to find a story that supports your message and resonates with your listeners. You can use personal stories, anecdotes, case studies, metaphors, analogies, or historical examples, as long as they are relevant to the topic and appropriate for the context. You also want to choose a story that has a clear structure, with a beginning, a middle, and an end, and that follows a classic narrative arc, with a protagonist, a challenge, a resolution, and a lesson learned.

3) **Craft your story with key elements.** After you have selected your story, you need to craft it with some key elements that make it engaging and impactful. These elements include:

   - **A hook:** This is the opening sentence or paragraph that grabs the attention of your audience and sets the tone for the rest of the story. You can use a question, a quote, a statistic, a surprising fact, or an intriguing scenario to spark curiosity and interest.
   - **A context:** This is the background information that sets the scene for your story and helps your audience understand the situation and the stakes. You can use details such as time, place, characters, and events to create a vivid picture of the setting and the problem.
   - **A conflict:** This is the main challenge or obstacle that the protagonist faces in the story and that creates tension and suspense. You can use dialogue, action, emotion, and sensory details to show how the protagonist struggles with the conflict and how it affects them.
   - **A climax:** This is the turning point or the peak of the story where the protagonist overcomes the conflict or learns something important. You can use contrast, surprise, humor, or irony to highlight the change or the insight that occurs in this moment.

21

- A resolution: This is the outcome or the consequence of the story where the protagonist achieves their goal or faces a new reality. You can use reflection, evaluation, or implication to show how the story ends and what it means for the protagonist and the audience.
- A call to action: This is the final sentence or paragraph that connects your story to your message and your audience and that invites them to take action or apply what they learned. You can use repetition, reinforcement, or recommendation to summarize your main point and suggest what your audience should do next.

4) Deliver your story with confidence and passion. After you have written your story, you need to practice it and deliver it with confidence and passion. You can use vocal variety, body language, eye contact, gestures, and facial expressions to enhance your delivery and convey emotion and enthusiasm. You also want to adapt your story to the situation and the feedback from your audience. You can modify your language, tone, pace, volume, or length depending on the context and the response from your listeners.

Storytelling is not only an art but also a skill that can be learned and improved with practice. By following these steps and applying storytelling techniques to your own situations and challenges, you can influence others more effectively and achieve your goals.

22

CHAPTER 4: The Art of Framing

One of the most important skills in the art of influence is framing. Framing is the way you present your message, your idea, your offer, or your request to your audience. Framing can make a huge difference in how your message is perceived, understood, and accepted. Framing can also help you overcome objections, create rapport, and build trust.

Framing is not about lying, manipulating, or deceiving. It is about choosing the best way to communicate your message in a way that resonates with your audience's values, beliefs, emotions, and needs. Framing is about highlighting the benefits, minimizing the drawbacks, and addressing the concerns of your audience. Framing is about using the right words, the right tone, the right examples, and the right stories to convey your message.

There are different types of framing that you can use to influence others. We will explore some of the most common and effective ones:

- **Positive vs. Negative Framing:** This is about emphasizing the positive or negative aspects of your message. For example, you can say "This product will save you $100 a month" or "If you don't buy this product, you will lose $100 a month". Both statements are true, but they have different emotional impacts on your audience. Positive framing tends to be more persuasive and appealing, while negative framing tends to be more alarming and urgent.

- **Gain vs. Loss Framing:** This is about focusing on what your audience can gain or lose by accepting or rejecting your message. For example, you can say "If you join our program, you will gain access to exclusive resources and opportunities" or "If you don't join our program, you will

23

miss out on exclusive resources and opportunities". Both statements are true, but they have different motivational effects on your audience. Gain framing tends to be more attractive and inspiring, while loss framing tends to be more compelling and persuasive.

- **Opportunity vs. Threat Framing:** This is about presenting your message as an opportunity or a threat for your audience. For example, you can say "This is a great opportunity for you to grow your business and reach new customers" or "This is a serious threat for your business and you need to act fast to avoid losing customers". Both statements are true, but they have different implications for your audience. Opportunity framing tends to be more optimistic and encouraging, while threat framing tends to be more pessimistic and alarming.

- **Solution vs. Problem Framing:** This is about showing how your message can solve a problem or create a problem for your audience. For example, you can say "This service will solve your problem of low productivity and high stress" or "If you don't use this service, you will have a problem of low productivity and high stress". Both statements are true, but they have different orientations for your audience. Solution framing tends to be more positive and helpful, while problem framing tends to be more negative and challenging.

- **Future vs. Present Framing:** This is about projecting how your message will affect the future or the present of your audience. For example, you can say "This investment will secure your future and give you peace of mind" or "This investment will improve your present and give you satisfaction". Both statements are true, but they have different time perspectives for your audience. Future framing tends to be more visionary and aspirational, while present framing tends to be more realistic and practical.

The key to using framing effectively is to know your audience well and understand their preferences, goals, fears, and values. You also need to adapt your framing according to the context, the situation, and the purpose of your message. You need to use framing ethically and responsibly, not to manipulate or coerce others, but to persuade and inspire them.

Framing is an art that requires practice and experimentation. The more you use it, the better you will become at it. Framing can help you become a master influencer who can communicate with clarity, confidence, and impact.

24

CHAPTER 5: The Skill of Questioning

One of the most important skills for any influencer is the ability to ask effective questions. Questions are powerful tools that can help you achieve various goals, such as:

- Building rapport and trust with your audience
- Discovering their needs, wants, problems, and motivations
- Uncovering their objections and concerns
- Guiding them to your desired outcome
- Persuading them to take action

However, not all questions are created equal. Some questions can enhance your influence, while others can diminish it. Some questions can open up the conversation, while others can shut it down. Some questions can elicit positive emotions, while others can trigger negative ones.

Therefore, you need to master the art and science of questioning, which involves knowing:

- What types of questions to ask
- When to ask them
- How to ask them
- How to listen to the answers

In this chapter, we will explore these aspects of questioning and provide you with some practical tips and examples on how to use questions effectively in your influence attempts.

Types of Questions

Questions can be classified into different types based on their purpose, structure, and scope. Here are some of the most common types of questions and how they can be used in influence situations:

1) **Open-ended questions:** These are questions that cannot be answered with a simple yes or no, but require a more elaborate response. They usually start with words like who, what, where, when, why, and how. For example:

   - What are your goals for this project?
   - How do you feel about the current situation?
   - Why did you choose this option?

   Open-ended questions are useful for:

   - Gathering information and insights from your audience
   - Encouraging them to express their thoughts and feelings
   - Showing interest and curiosity in their perspective
   - Stimulating their imagination and creativity

2) **Closed-ended questions:** These are questions that can be answered with a simple yes or no, or a short factual response. They usually start with words like do, did, are, is, can, will, and have. For example:

   - Do you have any questions?
   - Are you satisfied with the service?
   - Can you meet the deadline?

   Closed-ended questions are useful for:

   - Confirming or verifying information from your audience
   - Testing their knowledge or understanding
   - Making them commit to a decision or action
   - Closing the conversation or moving to the next step

3) **Probing questions:** These are questions that follow up on a previous question or answer to dig deeper into the topic. They usually start with

26

words like tell me more, could you explain, what do you mean by, and how so. For example:

- Tell me more about your challenges.
- Could you explain how this works?
- What do you mean by that?
- How so?

Probing questions are useful for:

- Clarifying or expanding on the information from your audience
- Exploring their underlying assumptions or beliefs
- Revealing their hidden motives or interests
- Challenging their logic or reasoning

4) **Leading questions:** These are questions that suggest or imply a desired answer or outcome. They usually start with words like don't you think, wouldn't you agree, isn't it true that, and wouldn't it be better if. For example:

- Don't you think this is a great opportunity?
- Wouldn't you agree that this is the best solution?
- Isn't it true that you need this product?
- Wouldn't it be better if you acted now?

Leading questions are useful for:

- Influencing the opinions or attitudes of your audience
- Persuading them to accept your point of view or proposal
- Creating a sense of urgency or scarcity
- Overcoming their objections or resistance

5) **Rhetorical questions:** These are questions that do not require an answer from your audience, but are used to make a statement or emphasize a point. They usually start with words like what if, how come, why not, and what's stopping you. For example:

- What if you could achieve your goals faster and easier?

27

- How come you haven't tried this before?
- Why not give it a try?
- What's stopping you from taking action?

Rhetorical questions are useful for:

- Capturing the attention or interest of your audience
- Engaging their emotions or curiosity
- Provoking their thoughts or reactions
- Motivating them to take action

Each type of question has its advantages and disadvantages depending on the context and goal of your influence attempt. Therefore, you need to choose wisely which type of question to use and when.

When to Ask Questions

Questions can be asked at different stages of the influence process, depending on what you want to achieve. Here are some general guidelines on when to ask questions:

- Before the influence attempt: You can ask questions to prepare yourself and your audience for the influence attempt. For example, you can ask questions to:

  - Research your audience and their needs, wants, problems, and motivations
  - Identify their decision criteria and preferences
  - Establish rapport and trust with them
  - Set the agenda and expectations for the conversation

- During the influence attempt: You can ask questions to guide and persuade your audience throughout the influence attempt. For example, you can ask questions to:

  - Explore their situation and challenges
  - Educate them about your solution and its benefits
  - Elicit their feedback and objections
  - Encourage them to commit and take action

28

- After the influence attempt: You can ask questions to follow up and reinforce your influence attempt. For example, you can ask questions to:

  - Confirm their satisfaction and results
  - Solicit their referrals and testimonials
  - Strengthen your relationship and loyalty
  - Create opportunities for future influence

By asking questions at the right time, you can increase your chances of success and avoid potential pitfalls in your influence attempt.

How to Ask Questions

The way you ask questions can also affect the quality and impact of your influence attempt. Here are some tips on how to ask questions effectively:

- **Be clear and concise:** Your questions should be easy to understand and answer. Avoid using jargon, ambiguity, or complexity that might confuse or overwhelm your audience. Use simple and direct language that matches their level of knowledge and interest.

- **Be relevant and focused:** Your questions should be related to the topic and goal of your influence attempt. Avoid asking irrelevant or random questions that might distract or bore your audience. Use specific and targeted questions that address their needs, wants, problems, and motivations.

- **Be respectful and polite:** Your questions should be respectful of your audience's time, privacy, and feelings. Avoid asking intrusive or offensive questions that might annoy or upset your audience. Use courteous and considerate language that shows your appreciation and empathy.

- **Be flexible and adaptable:** Your questions should be flexible enough to adapt to the situation and the response of your audience. Avoid asking rigid or scripted questions that might limit or constrain your audience. Use open-ended and probing questions that allow for exploration and discovery.

How to Listen to the Answers

29

Asking questions is only half of the equation. The other half is listening to the answers. Listening is a crucial skill for any influencer, as it can help you:

- Understand your audience better
- Build rapport and trust with them
- Identify their needs, wants, problems, and motivations
- Uncover their objections and concerns
- Guide them to your desired outcome
- Persuade them to take action

However, listening is not as easy as it sounds. Many people tend to listen poorly or selectively, which can undermine their influence attempts. Here are some tips on how to listen effectively:

- **Be attentive and engaged:** You should pay attention to what your audience is saying, as well as how they are saying it. Observe their verbal cues (such as words, tone, pace, etc.) and non-verbal cues (such as facial expressions, body language, eye contact, etc.) that might indicate their emotions, attitudes, or intentions. Show interest and enthusiasm in their responses by nodding, smiling, or making appropriate comments.

- **Be active and responsive:** You should not just listen passively, but actively participate in the conversation. Ask follow-up questions to clarify or expand on their answers. Provide feedback or acknowledgment to show that you understand or agree with them. Summarize or paraphrase their key points to confirm or reinforce them.

- **Be open-minded and curious:** You should not listen with a preconceived notion or agenda, but with an open mind and curiosity. Do not judge or criticize their answers, but respect their perspective and experience. Do not interrupt or argue with them, but listen patiently and respectfully. Do not assume or guess what they mean, but ask for clarification or examples.

Conclusion

Questions are powerful tools that can help you influence others effectively. By mastering the art and science of questioning, you can:

30

- Build rapport and trust with your audience
- Discover their needs, wants, problems, and motivations
- Uncover their objections and concerns
- Guide them to your desired outcome
- Persuade them to take action

However, not all questions are created equal. You need to know what types of questions to ask, when to ask them, how to ask them, and how to listen to the answers.

In this chapter, we have provided you with some practical tips and examples on how to use questions effectively in your influence attempts.

In the next chapter, we will explore another important skill for any influencer: the strategy of listening.

31

CHAPTER 6: The Strategy of Listening

One of the most important and often overlooked skills in influence is listening. Listening is not just a passive act of receiving information, but an active process of engaging with the speaker, understanding their perspective, and building rapport and trust. Listening is also a way of showing respect, empathy, and curiosity, which are essential for creating positive and lasting impressions.

In this chapter, we will explore the benefits of listening, the barriers that prevent us from listening effectively, and the techniques that can help us improve our listening skills. We will also learn how to use listening as a strategic tool to influence others in various situations.

The Benefits of Listening

Listening has many benefits for both the listener and the speaker. Some of the benefits are:

- **Listening helps us learn.** By listening attentively, we can gain new knowledge, insights, and perspectives from others. We can also discover the needs, wants, goals, values, and motivations of others, which can help us tailor our messages and offers accordingly.

- **Listening helps us solve problems.** By listening carefully, we can understand the root causes of problems, identify potential solutions, and avoid misunderstandings and conflicts. We can also generate creative ideas and innovations by listening to diverse opinions and perspectives.

- **Listening helps us persuade.** By listening actively, we can establish rapport and trust with others, which are crucial for influencing them. We

32

can also identify common ground and areas of agreement, which can help us build bridges and alliances. We can also uncover objections and concerns, which can help us address them effectively.

- **Listening helps us inspire.** By listening empathetically, we can show genuine interest and care for others, which can make them feel valued and appreciated. We can also acknowledge their emotions and feelings, which can help them feel understood and supported. We can also express appreciation and recognition, which can help them feel motivated and inspired.

The Barriers to Listening

Despite the benefits of listening, many of us struggle to listen effectively. There are many barriers that prevent us from listening well. Some of the barriers are:

- **Distractions.** We live in a noisy and busy world, where we are constantly bombarded by stimuli and information. It is easy to get distracted by external factors such as noises, interruptions, or devices, or by internal factors such as thoughts, emotions, or biases. Distractions can reduce our attention span and focus, and make us miss important details or cues.

- **Assumptions.** We often make assumptions about what others are saying or thinking based on our own experiences, beliefs, or expectations. We may think that we already know what they are going to say or that we have heard it before. We may also judge or evaluate what they are saying based on our own standards or criteria. Assumptions can prevent us from listening with an open mind and curiosity, and make us miss opportunities to learn or discover something new.

- **Interruptions.** We sometimes interrupt others while they are speaking because we want to express our opinions, share our stories, give advice, or correct them. We may think that we are being helpful or supportive, but we may actually be showing disrespect or impatience. Interruptions can break the flow of communication and damage the rapport and trust between us and the speaker.

- **Defensiveness.** We sometimes react defensively when we hear something that challenges our views, values, or interests. We may feel threatened or attacked by what others are saying or implying. We may respond with

33

arguments, counterattacks, excuses, or denials. Defensiveness can create resistance and conflict between us and the speaker, and prevent us from listening with empathy and understanding.

The Techniques for Listening

To overcome the barriers to listening and to listen effectively, we need to practice some techniques that can help us improve our listening skills. Some of the techniques are:

- **Prepare to listen.** Before engaging in a conversation or a meeting where we need to listen carefully, we need to prepare ourselves mentally and physically. We need to clear our mind from distractions and preconceptions, and focus on the purpose and goal of listening. We also need to create a conducive environment for listening by eliminating or minimizing noises, interruptions, or devices that may distract us or the speaker.

- **Pay attention to the speaker.** While listening to someone speak, we need to pay attention not only to what they are saying but also to how they are saying it. We need to observe their body language, tone of voice, facial expressions, eye contact, gestures, and other nonverbal cues that may convey their emotions, attitudes, intentions, or meanings. We also need to show that we are paying attention by using appropriate nonverbal cues ourselves, such as nodding, smiling, leaning forward, or maintaining eye contact.

- **Ask open-ended questions.** One of the best ways to show interest and curiosity while listening is to ask open-ended questions that invite the speaker to elaborate, clarify, explain, or give examples of what they are saying. Open-ended questions usually start with words such as who, what, where, when, why, or how, and cannot be answered with a simple yes or no. For example, instead of asking "Do you like your job?", we can ask "What do you like about your job?" or "How did you get into your field of work?"

- **Paraphrase and summarize.** Another way to show understanding and respect while listening is to paraphrase and summarize what the speaker has said in our own words. Paraphrasing is repeating the main points or ideas of what the speaker has said using different words or expressions.

34

Summarizing is condensing the main points or ideas of what the speaker has said into a brief statement or conclusion. Paraphrasing and summarizing can help us check our comprehension and accuracy, as well as confirm or clarify the speaker's message. For example, after listening to someone talk about their vacation, we can paraphrase by saying "So you had a great time in Hawaii, enjoying the beach, the food, and the culture." We can also summarize by saying "It sounds like you had a wonderful vacation that you will always remember."

- **Provide feedback.** The final step in listening effectively is to provide feedback to the speaker that shows our appreciation, recognition, or evaluation of what they have said. Feedback can be positive or negative, depending on the situation and the goal of listening. Positive feedback can include compliments, praise, agreement, support, or encouragement. Negative feedback can include criticism, disagreement, advice, or suggestions. Feedback should be honest, specific, timely, and constructive. For example, after listening to someone present their project, we can provide positive feedback by saying "That was a very impressive presentation. You did a great job of explaining the problem, the solution, and the benefits." We can also provide negative feedback by saying "I liked your presentation, but I think you need to work on your delivery. You spoke too fast, too softly, and too monotonously."

The Strategy of Listening

Listening is not only a skill but also a strategy that we can use to influence others in various situations. By listening effectively, we can achieve different outcomes depending on our purpose and goal. Some of the situations where we can use listening as a strategy are:

- **To build rapport and trust.** When we want to establish or strengthen a relationship with someone, we need to listen to them with interest and empathy. We need to show that we care about them as a person, not just as a source of information or a means to an end. We need to listen to their stories, experiences, feelings, and opinions without judging or interrupting them. We need to make them feel valued and appreciated for who they are and what they have to say.

- **To persuade and influence.** When we want to persuade or influence someone to do something or to agree with us, we need to listen to them

35

with respect and curiosity. We need to show that we understand their perspective, needs, wants, goals, values, and motivations. We need to listen to their objections and concerns without arguing or attacking them. We need to make them feel heard and understood before presenting our own views or proposals.

- **To learn and discover.** When we want to learn or discover something new from someone, we need to listen to them with openness and eagerness. We need to show that we are willing to learn from their knowledge, insights, or perspectives. We need to listen to their facts, arguments, evidence, or examples without assuming or interrupting them. We need to make them feel respected and recognized for their expertise or experience.

- **To solve problems and innovate.** When we want to solve problems or innovate with someone, we need to listen to them with collaboration and creativity. We need to show that we are interested in their ideas, suggestions, or solutions. We need to listen to their challenges, opportunities, or feedback without dismissing or rejecting them. We need to make them feel involved and appreciated for their contribution or input.

Conclusion

Listening is one of the most powerful and essential skills in influence. Listening is not just a passive act of receiving information, but an active process of engaging with the speaker, understanding their perspective, and building rapport and trust. Listening is also a way of showing respect, empathy, and curiosity, which are vital for creating positive and lasting impressions.

In this chapter, we have explored the benefits of listening, the barriers that prevent us from listening effectively, and the techniques that can help us improve our listening skills. We have also learned how to use listening as a strategic tool to influence others in various situations.

By practicing and applying these techniques and strategies, we can become better listeners and better influencers. We can also become better learners, problem solvers, and innovators.

<u>Remember: The art of influence begins with the art of listening.</u>

36

CHAPTER 7: The Technique of Mirroring

Have you ever noticed how some people seem to have a natural rapport with others? How they can easily connect and communicate with anyone, regardless of their background, personality, or preferences? How they can make others feel comfortable and understood, without even saying much?

One of the secrets behind this skill is the technique of mirroring. Mirroring is the subtle and unconscious act of mimicking the verbal and non-verbal cues of another person, such as their tone of voice, body language, facial expressions, gestures, words, and phrases. By doing so, you create a sense of similarity and familiarity with the other person, which in turn fosters trust, empathy, and rapport.

Mirroring is a powerful technique of influence because it taps into one of the most fundamental human needs: the need to belong. We are social animals who crave connection and acceptance from others. We tend to like and trust people who are like us, who share our values, beliefs, opinions, and interests. We also tend to avoid and distrust people who are different from us, who challenge our views, or who threaten our identity.

By mirroring the other person, you signal that you are one of them, that you understand them, and that you respect them. You also reduce the perceived distance and difference between you and them, which makes them more open and receptive to your ideas and suggestions. You create a positive feedback loop that reinforces the bond and the influence between you.

But how do you use mirroring effectively? Here are some tips and guidelines to help you master this technique:

37

- **Be subtle and natural.** Don't overdo it or make it obvious that you are copying the other person. That would be creepy and counterproductive. Instead, mirror only a few aspects of their behavior at a time, and do it in a smooth and natural way. For example, if they lean forward slightly, you can lean forward slightly too. If they use a certain word or phrase frequently, you can use it occasionally too. If they speak slowly and softly, you can lower your voice and pace too.

- **Be selective and appropriate.** Don't mirror everything the other person does or says. That would be robotic and insincere. Instead, mirror only what is relevant and appropriate for the context and the goal of your interaction. For example, if they are angry or upset, don't mirror their negative emotions or expressions. That would only escalate the situation and damage the relationship. Instead, mirror their positive emotions or expressions when they calm down or show signs of agreement or cooperation.

- **Be flexible and adaptive.** Don't mirror the other person blindly or rigidly. That would be ineffective and insensitive. Instead, mirror them with awareness and sensitivity to their reactions and feedback. For example, if they change their posture or tone of voice, you can change yours too. If they seem uncomfortable or resistant to your mirroring, you can stop or adjust it accordingly.

- **Be genuine and respectful.** Don't mirror the other person manipulatively or disrespectfully. That would be unethical and risky. Instead, mirror them with honesty and respect for their individuality and dignity. For example, don't mirror them to deceive them or exploit them for your own benefit. Don't mirror them to mock them or make fun of them. Don't mirror them to impose your views or values on them.

Mirroring is a technique that can help you build rapport and influence with anyone, but only if you use it wisely and ethically. Remember that mirroring is not a magic trick that can make anyone do anything you want. It is a tool that can enhance your communication and relationship with others, but only if you use it with care and integrity.

38

CHAPTER 8: The Method of Reciprocity

One of the most powerful ways to influence someone is to use the method of reciprocity. Reciprocity is the tendency to return a favor or a gesture that someone has done for us. It is based on the principle of mutual exchange and fairness. When someone does something nice for us, we feel obliged to do something nice for them in return. This creates a bond of trust and goodwill between us and the other person.

Reciprocity can be used to persuade, negotiate and inspire others in various situations. For example, if you want someone to buy your product or service, you can offer them a free sample, a discount or a bonus. This will make them more likely to buy from you, because they will feel that they owe you something. If you want someone to agree with your proposal or idea, you can compliment them, acknowledge their point of view or concede a minor point. This will make them more likely to agree with you, because they will feel that you are reasonable and respectful. If you want someone to help you with a task or a project, you can help them first, thank them sincerely or offer them something in return. This will make them more likely to help you, because they will feel that you are generous and appreciative.

However, reciprocity is not a simple tit-for-tat exchange. It is a subtle and nuanced art that requires careful planning and execution. Here are some tips on how to use reciprocity effectively:

- **Be the first to give.** Don't wait for the other person to do something for you before you do something for them. Take the initiative and be proactive. This will create a positive impression and set the tone for the interaction.

39

- **Give something of value.** Don't give something cheap or trivial that the other person doesn't need or want. Give something that is relevant, useful and meaningful to them. This will increase their satisfaction and gratitude.

- **Give something unexpected.** Don't give something predictable or obvious that the other person expects or demands. Give something surprising or extra that goes beyond their expectations. This will increase their curiosity and interest.

- **Give something personalized.** Don't give something generic or impersonal that anyone can get. Give something specific or customized that reflects their preferences, needs or goals. This will increase their connection and loyalty.

- **Give without strings attached.** Don't give something with a hidden agenda or a condition that the other person has to fulfill. Give something freely and genuinely without expecting anything in return. This will increase their respect and admiration.

Reciprocity is a powerful method of influence that can help you achieve your goals and build lasting relationships with others. By giving first, giving value, giving unexpectedly, giving personally and giving unconditionally, you can create a positive cycle of mutual benefit and cooperation.

40

CHAPTER 9: The Tool of Scarcity

One of the most powerful tools of influence is scarcity. Scarcity is the perception that something is rare, limited, or in high demand. Scarcity creates a sense of urgency, fear of missing out, and desire to obtain the scarce resource. Scarcity can be used to influence people's decisions, behaviors, and emotions in various situations.

In this chapter, we will explore how scarcity works, why it is effective, and how to use it ethically and strategically to persuade, negotiate, and inspire others. We will also examine some of the pitfalls and challenges of using scarcity, and how to avoid them.

How Scarcity Works

Scarcity works by activating two psychological principles: reactance and value attribution.

Reactance is the tendency to resist or oppose any perceived threat to our freedom or autonomy. When something is scarce, we feel that our freedom to choose or obtain it is threatened or restricted. This triggers a negative emotional reaction, such as anger, frustration, or anxiety. This reaction motivates us to act quickly to restore our freedom and reduce the negative emotion. For example, if you see a sign that says "Last chance to buy", you may feel a sense of urgency and pressure to buy the product before it runs out.

Value attribution is the tendency to assign more value or importance to something that is scarce or difficult to obtain. When something is scarce, we assume that it is more valuable, desirable, or attractive than something that is abundant or easy to obtain. This is because we use scarcity as a cue or heuristic to judge the quality or

41

worth of something. For example, if you see a product that has a limited edition label, you may assume that it is more special, exclusive, or superior than a regular product.

Why Scarcity Is Effective

Scarcity is effective because it influences both our rational and emotional systems. On one hand, scarcity appeals to our rational system by providing logical reasons or evidence to support our decision or action. For example, if you see a product that has a 50% discount for a limited time only, you may think that it is a good deal and a smart choice to buy it now.

On the other hand, scarcity appeals to our emotional system by creating emotional arousal and excitement. For example, if you see a product that has only one left in stock, you may feel a thrill and a challenge to get it before someone else does.

Scarcity also exploits our cognitive biases and heuristics, such as loss aversion, anchoring, and social proof. Loss aversion is the tendency to prefer avoiding losses over acquiring gains. When something is scarce, we focus more on what we might lose than what we might gain. For example, if you see a product that has a countdown timer showing how much time is left before the offer expires, you may feel more pain from missing the opportunity than pleasure from getting the product.

Anchoring is the tendency to rely on the first piece of information we receive as a reference point for making subsequent judgments or decisions. When something is scarce, we use the original price or quantity as an anchor to compare with the current price or quantity. For example, if you see a product that has a 70% discount from its original price of $1000, you may think that it is a bargain and ignore other factors such as quality or utility.

Social proof is the tendency to follow the behavior or opinions of others, especially when we are uncertain or in ambiguous situations. When something is scarce, we assume that it is popular or in high demand by others. This increases our trust and confidence in the product or service. For example, if you see a product that has a lot of positive reviews or testimonials from other customers, you may think that it is more credible and reliable than a product that has few or no reviews.

42

CHAPTER 10: The Factor of Authority

One of the most powerful ways to influence others is to leverage the factor of authority. Authority is the perception that someone has the right, the expertise, or the credibility to make decisions, give orders, or provide guidance. People tend to obey and trust those who have authority, even if they don't agree with them or like them. Authority can be based on various sources, such as position, reputation, experience, knowledge, credentials, or appearance. In this chapter, we will explore how you can use authority to persuade, negotiate, and inspire others.

The first step to using authority is to establish your own authority. This means that you need to demonstrate that you have the qualifications, the skills, the results, or the recognition that make you an authority in your field or domain. You can do this by highlighting your achievements, showcasing your testimonials, displaying your awards, citing your references, or sharing your stories. You can also use symbols of authority, such as titles, uniforms, badges, logos, or certificates. However, be careful not to overdo it or brag about it, as this can backfire and make you seem arrogant or insecure.

The second step to using authority is to borrow authority from others. This means that you can leverage the authority of someone else who is more influential, more respected, or more credible than you. You can do this by associating yourself with them, quoting them, endorsing them, or getting their endorsement. You can also use sources of authority, such as books, articles, studies, statistics, or experts. However, be sure to use relevant and reliable sources of authority that support your message and your audience.

The third step to using authority is to give authority to others. This means that you can empower others to feel more confident, more capable, or more motivated by

43

granting them authority. You can do this by delegating tasks, assigning roles, giving feedback, offering praise, or providing incentives. You can also use techniques of authority, such as pre-suasion, social validation, or scarcity. However, be mindful not to abuse your authority or manipulate others with it, as this can damage your trust and reputation.

The factor of authority is a potent influence tool that can help you achieve your goals and make a positive impact on others. By establishing your own authority, borrowing authority from others, and giving authority to others, you can enhance your persuasiveness, your negotiation skills, and your inspirational abilities. Remember that authority is not only about having power over others but also about using power for good.

44

CHAPTER 11: The Role of Social Proof

Social proof is the phenomenon where people look to the actions and opinions of others to guide their own behavior. It is based on the assumption that if many people are doing something or believing something, it must be right or good. Social proof is a powerful influence technique because it taps into our natural desire to fit in and conform to social norms.

One of the most famous experiments on social proof was conducted by psychologist Stanley Milgram in the 1960s. He had a group of actors stand on a busy street corner and look up at the sky. As more and more actors joined them, more and more passersby also stopped and looked up, even though there was nothing to see. This showed how easily people can be influenced by the actions of others, even without any explanation or reason.

Social proof can be used in various ways to persuade, negotiate and inspire others. Here are some examples:

- **Testimonials and reviews:** When we want to buy a product or service, we often look for the opinions of other customers who have used it before. Testimonials and reviews provide social proof that the product or service is valuable, reliable and satisfying. They also create a sense of trust and credibility for the seller or provider. Therefore, if you want to sell something, you should collect and display positive testimonials and reviews from your previous or current customers.

- **Endorsements and referrals:** When we want to choose a professional or an expert, we often look for the recommendations of other people who have worked with them before. Endorsements and referrals provide social proof that the professional or expert is competent, experienced and

45

reputable. They also create a sense of authority and legitimacy for the professional or expert. Therefore, if you want to promote yourself or someone else, you should seek and share endorsements and referrals from your previous or current clients, colleagues or partners.

- **Social media and online platforms:** When we want to learn something new or get inspired, we often look for the content and messages of other people who have similar interests or goals. Social media and online platforms provide social proof that the content and messages are relevant, useful and engaging. They also create a sense of community and belonging for the users. Therefore, if you want to educate or inspire others, you should create and share content and messages that attract and retain followers, subscribers, likes, comments and shares.

- **Awards and recognition:** When we want to achieve something great or make a difference, we often look for the achievements and contributions of other people who have done it before. Awards and recognition provide social proof that the achievements and contributions are significant, impactful and admirable. They also create a sense of admiration and aspiration for the achievers and contributors. Therefore, if you want to motivate or influence others, you should highlight and celebrate awards and recognition that you or others have received or given.

Social proof is a valuable tool for influencing others, but it also has some limitations and risks. Here are some things to keep in mind:

- **Quality over quantity:** Not all social proof is equally persuasive. The quality of the source, the relevance of the context, and the credibility of the evidence are important factors that affect how much social proof influences us. For example, we are more likely to trust the opinion of an expert than a stranger, the feedback of a similar customer than a different one, and the data of a reputable organization than an unknown one. Therefore, you should focus on providing high-quality social proof rather than just a large quantity of it.

- **Diversity over uniformity:** Not all people are influenced by social proof in the same way. The personality, preferences, values and goals of the individual are important factors that affect how much social proof influences them. For example, some people are more independent and skeptical than others, some people are more attracted to novelty than

46

familiarity, some people are more aligned with their own group than other groups. Therefore, you should tailor your social proof to match the needs and wants of your target audience rather than assuming they are all alike.

- **Ethics over manipulation:** Not all social proof is ethical or truthful. Some people may use fake or misleading social proof to deceive or coerce others into doing something they don't want to do or shouldn't do. For example, some people may fabricate testimonials or reviews, pay for endorsements or referrals, buy followers or likes, or claim awards or recognition they don't deserve. Therefore, you should use social proof with honesty and integrity rather than with dishonesty and manipulation.

Social proof is a key factor that influences our decisions and actions. By understanding how it works and how to use it effectively, you can enhance your ability to persuade, negotiate and inspire others.

47

CHAPTER 12: The Element of Liking

One of the most powerful factors that can influence people's decisions and actions is how much they like the person who is trying to persuade them. Liking is a subjective feeling of attraction, affinity, or rapport that can be based on various factors, such as appearance, personality, similarity, compliments, cooperation, or association. In this chapter, we will explore how to use the element of liking to increase your influence and persuade others more effectively.

The first thing to understand about liking is that it is not a fixed or objective quality. It is a dynamic and relative perception that can change depending on the context and the situation. For example, you may like someone more if you see them in a positive light, such as when they help you, praise you, or share something in common with you. Conversely, you may like someone less if you see them in a negative light, such as when they criticize you, compete with you, or disagree with you.

Therefore, one of the keys to using liking as an influence tool is to create positive impressions and associations with yourself and your message. You want to make people feel good about you and what you are offering, so that they will be more likely to listen to you and comply with your requests. Here are some ways to do that:

- **Use physical attractiveness.** Research has shown that people tend to like and trust those who are physically attractive more than those who are not. This does not mean that you have to be a supermodel or a movie star to be influential, but it does mean that you should pay attention to your appearance and grooming, and dress appropriately for the occasion. You should also use nonverbal cues, such as eye contact, smiling, nodding, and leaning forward, to convey warmth and interest.

48

- **Use similarity.** People also tend to like and trust those who are similar to them in some way, such as having the same background, values, opinions, interests, hobbies, or preferences. This is because similarity creates a sense of familiarity and connection, and reduces the perceived distance and difference between people. You can use similarity to increase your likability by finding out what you have in common with your audience, and highlighting those aspects in your communication. You can also use language, jargon, slang, or humor that matches their style and level of formality.

- **Use compliments.** Another way to make people like you more is to give them sincere and specific compliments. Compliments are expressions of admiration or appreciation that can boost people's self-esteem and make them feel good about themselves. When you compliment someone, you are also implying that you like them and value them. However, you have to be careful not to overdo it or sound insincere, as this can backfire and make people suspicious or resentful of your motives. You should also avoid complimenting yourself or comparing yourself favorably to others, as this can come across as arrogant or boastful.

- **Use cooperation.** A fourth way to increase your likability is to cooperate with others and work toward a common goal. Cooperation creates a sense of teamwork and solidarity, and fosters positive feelings of trust and loyalty. When you cooperate with someone, you are also signaling that you share their interests and values, and that you are willing to help them achieve their desired outcomes. You can use cooperation to enhance your influence by finding out what your audience wants and needs, and showing how your message or proposal can benefit them or solve their problems. You can also offer assistance or support when needed, or ask for their input or feedback.

- **Use association.** A final way to use liking as an influence tool is to associate yourself or your message with something or someone that your audience already likes or respects. Association is a psychological phenomenon that links two stimuli together based on their proximity or similarity. For example, if you see a product endorsed by a celebrity that you admire, you may be more inclined to buy it because of the positive association between the product and the celebrity. You can use association

49

to increase your likability by linking yourself or your message with a person, group, brand, event, or idea that your audience likes or respects.

These are some of the ways that you can use the element of liking to increase your influence and persuade others more effectively. By creating positive impressions and associations with yourself and your message, you can make people feel good about you and what you are offering, and increase their willingness to listen to you and comply with your requests.

However, as with any other influence technique, you have to use liking ethically and responsibly. You should not use liking to manipulate people into doing something that is against their best interests or values. You should also not use liking to deceive people or hide important information from them. You should always be honest and respectful of others' opinions and preferences.

Remember that liking is not only an influence tool but also a genuine human emotion that can enrich your relationships and interactions with others. By using liking appropriately and authentically, you can not only become a more influential person, but also a more likable one.

50

CHAPTER 13: The Concept of Commitment and Consistency

One of the most powerful ways to influence someone is to make them commit to something and then help them stay consistent with their commitment. Commitment and consistency are psychological principles that explain why people tend to act in ways that are aligned with their previous decisions, statements, or actions.

When people commit to something, they feel a sense of obligation and responsibility to follow through. They also want to avoid the cognitive dissonance that arises from behaving inconsistently with their beliefs, values, or self-image. Commitment and consistency can be used to influence others by creating situations where they are more likely to agree to a request or a proposal that is congruent with their prior commitments.

In this chapter, we will explore how to use commitment and consistency to persuade, negotiate, and inspire others. We will cover the following topics:

- How to elicit commitment from others by using small requests, public declarations, written agreements, or voluntary actions.
- How to increase consistency by using labels, reminders, incentives, or social norms.
- How to avoid being influenced by commitment and consistency by recognizing the tactics, questioning the motives, or changing your mind.

How to elicit commitment from others by using small requests, public declarations, written agreements, or voluntary actions

51

One of the most important skills in the context of influence is the ability to elicit commitment from others. Commitment is the psychological state of being bound or obligated to a course of action, especially one that is consistent with one's own values and beliefs. Commitment can increase the likelihood of compliance, cooperation, and persistence in pursuing a goal.

There are several strategies that can be used to elicit commitment from others, depending on the situation and the relationship between the parties. Here are some of them:

- **Small requests:** This strategy involves asking for a small favor or concession that is easy to agree to, and then gradually increasing the size or scope of the request until the desired outcome is achieved. This works because people tend to be consistent with their previous behavior and decisions, and they want to avoid cognitive dissonance (the uncomfortable feeling of holding contradictory beliefs or attitudes). For example, a salesperson might ask a potential customer to fill out a short survey, then offer a free sample, then suggest a trial period, and finally propose a purchase.

- **Public declarations:** This strategy involves asking someone to publicly state their intention or opinion on a matter, which makes them more likely to follow through with their words. This works because people care about their reputation and self-image, and they want to avoid social pressure or embarrassment. For example, a manager might ask an employee to announce their goals for the next quarter in front of their colleagues, which would motivate them to work harder and achieve them.

- **Written agreements:** This strategy involves asking someone to sign a document or contract that formalizes their commitment to a certain action or outcome. This works because people tend to honor their written promises and obligations, and they want to avoid legal consequences or penalties. For example, a landlord might ask a tenant to sign a lease agreement that specifies the terms and conditions of renting a property, which would bind them to pay rent on time and follow the rules.

- **Voluntary actions:** This strategy involves asking someone to voluntarily perform an action that implies their commitment to a cause or value, without explicitly requesting it. This works because people tend to infer their own attitudes and beliefs from their behavior, and they want to

52

maintain a positive self-concept. For example, a charity might ask a donor to wear a wristband or sticker that shows their support for a social issue, which would make them feel more committed to the cause and more likely to donate again.

By applying the concept of commitment and consistency, you will be able to influence others more effectively and ethically. You will also be able to strengthen your own commitment and consistency by aligning your actions with your goals and values.

How to increase consistency by using labels, reminders, incentives, or social norms

Consistency is the ability to act in accordance with one's values, beliefs, and commitments over time. It is an important factor for building trust, credibility, and influence. However, consistency can be challenging to maintain in a complex and dynamic world, where we face competing demands, changing circumstances, and conflicting information. How can we increase our consistency and align our actions with our intentions? In this article, we will explore four strategies that can help us achieve consistency: using labels, reminders, incentives, or social norms.

Labels are words or phrases that describe ourselves or others in a positive or negative way. They can influence how we perceive ourselves and how we behave towards others. For example, if we label ourselves as "responsible", "honest", or "reliable", we are more likely to act in ways that match those labels. Conversely, if we label ourselves as "lazy", "dishonest", or "unreliable", we are more likely to act in ways that contradict those labels. Labels can also affect how others perceive us and how they treat us. For example, if we label someone as "friendly", "helpful", or "trustworthy", we are more likely to cooperate with them and trust them. Conversely, if we label someone as "hostile", "selfish", or "untrustworthy", we are more likely to avoid them and distrust them.

To use labels effectively, we need to be aware of the labels we use for ourselves and others, and choose them carefully. We should avoid using labels that are negative, inaccurate, or inconsistent with our values and goals. We should also avoid using labels that are too general or vague, such as "good" or "bad". Instead, we should use labels that are positive, specific, and consistent with our values and goals. For example, instead of saying "I'm a good person", we could say "I'm a person who values honesty and kindness". This way, we can create a clear and positive self-image that guides our actions and reinforces our consistency.

53

Reminders are cues or signals that prompt us to recall our values, beliefs, and commitments. They can help us stay focused on our goals and avoid distractions or temptations. For example, if we want to exercise regularly, we could set an alarm on our phone, put our workout clothes near our bed, or join a fitness class with a friend. These reminders can help us remember why we want to exercise and motivate us to do it. Reminders can also help us overcome procrastination or inertia by creating a sense of urgency or accountability. For example, if we have a deadline for a project, we could write it on a calendar, post it on a bulletin board, or tell someone about it. These reminders can help us realize the importance of the project and push us to start working on it.

To use reminders effectively, we need to make them visible, frequent, and relevant. We should place them where we can see them often, such as on our desk, on our fridge, or on our mirror. We should also update them regularly to keep them fresh and interesting. For example, we could change the message on our phone alarm every week or use different colors for our calendar entries. We should also make sure that the reminders are related to our values, beliefs, and commitments. For example, if we want to exercise regularly because we value health and well-being, we could use a reminder that says "Exercise for your health" or "Exercise because you love yourself". This way, we can create a strong connection between the reminder and the goal and increase our consistency.

Incentives are external factors that can increase consistency by providing positive or negative consequences for a person's actions. For example, if a person wants to lose weight, they might use incentives such as buying new clothes, getting compliments, or avoiding health problems as reasons to stick to their diet and exercise plan. Incentives can also be used by others to persuade someone to act in a certain way. For example, a salesperson might offer discounts, bonuses, or guarantees to convince a customer to buy their product or service. Incentives can be effective because they appeal to people's self-interest and rationality.

However, incentives also have some limitations and drawbacks. First, incentives can be costly and time-consuming to implement and monitor. Second, incentives can lose their effectiveness over time as people get used to them or find ways to cheat or avoid them. Third, incentives can undermine people's intrinsic motivation and satisfaction, making them feel like they are doing something only for the reward or punishment, not because they enjoy it or believe in it. Fourth, incentives can create ethical dilemmas and conflicts of interest, especially when they involve money or other scarce resources.

54

Social norms are internal factors that can increase consistency by activating people's need for social approval and belonging. For example, if a person wants to quit smoking, they might use social norms such as joining a support group, following role models, or avoiding peer pressure as reasons to stick to their decision. Social norms can also be used by others to persuade someone to act in a certain way. For example, a charity might use social proof, such as testimonials, statistics, or endorsements, to show that many people have donated or supported their cause. Social norms can be effective because they appeal to people's emotions and identity.

However, social norms also have some limitations and drawbacks. First, social norms can be ambiguous and subjective, depending on the context and the audience. Second, social norms can change over time and across cultures, making them hard to predict and apply. Third, social norms can create conformity and compliance, making people act in ways that are not authentic or consistent with their true selves. Fourth, social norms can create resistance and backlash, especially when they are perceived as coercive or manipulative.

How to avoid being influenced by commitment and consistency by recognizing the tactics, questioning the motives, or changing your mind

One of the most powerful principles of influence is commitment and consistency. This means that once we make a choice or take a stand, we feel pressure to behave consistently with that commitment. This pressure can come from ourselves or from others who expect us to follow through on our word. Commitment and consistency can be useful tools for achieving our goals and staying true to our values, but they can also be exploited by those who want to manipulate us into doing something we might not otherwise do.

How can we avoid being influenced by commitment and consistency when it is not in our best interest? Here are some strategies to help you recognize the tactics, question the motives, and change your mind if necessary.

Recognize the tactics. Some common tactics that use commitment and consistency to influence us are:

- **The foot-in-the-door technique:** This involves asking for a small favor or agreement first, and then following up with a larger request that is consistent with the initial one. For example, a salesperson might ask you to sign a petition for a cause you support, and then ask you to buy a product that supports the same cause.

- **The low-ball technique:** This involves making an attractive offer at first, and then revealing hidden costs or drawbacks after you have agreed to it. For example, a car dealer might quote you a low price for a car, and then add fees, taxes, and extras after you have committed to buy it.

- **The bait-and-switch technique:** This involves presenting an appealing option at first, and then substituting it with a less desirable one after you have agreed to it. For example, a travel agent might offer you a cheap flight to your destination, and then tell you that it is sold out and offer you a more expensive one instead.

- **The label technique:** This involves assigning a positive label to yourself or someone else, and then asking for a favor or agreement that is consistent with that label. For example, a fundraiser might compliment you on being a generous person, and then ask you to donate money to their cause.

Question the motives. When someone tries to influence you using commitment and consistency, ask yourself:

- Why are they asking me to do this? What is their goal or agenda?
- Do they have my best interest at heart, or are they trying to benefit themselves or someone else at my expense?
- Are they being honest and transparent, or are they hiding something or misleading me?
- Do I really want to do this, or am I feeling pressured or obligated to do it?
- Is this consistent with my values, beliefs, and preferences, or am I compromising them?

Change your mind. If you realize that you have agreed to something that is not in your best interest, remember that you have the right to change your mind. You can do this by:

- **Saying no.** You can simply say that you have changed your mind and decline the offer or request. You do not owe anyone an explanation or apology for your decision.

56

- **Asking for more information.** You can ask for more details, evidence, or clarification before you make a final decision. You can also compare different options and alternatives to see which one suits you best.

- **Seeking a second opinion.** You can consult someone else who is trustworthy, knowledgeable, or experienced in the matter. You can also do your own research and verify the facts and claims yourself.

- **Negotiating a better deal.** You can try to modify the terms or conditions of the agreement to make it more favorable for you. You can also ask for something in return or exchange for your compliance.

Commitment and consistency are powerful forces that can influence our behavior, but they are not always beneficial for us. By recognizing the tactics, questioning the motives, and changing your mind if necessary, you can avoid being influenced by commitment and consistency when it is not in your best interest.

CHAPTER 14: The Model of Contrast

One of the most powerful ways to influence someone is to use the model of contrast. This is a technique that involves presenting two or more options or scenarios that are different in some aspect, such as quality, price, value, risk, benefit, etc. The purpose of using contrast is to make one option or scenario seem more attractive, desirable, or reasonable than the other(s).

The model of contrast works because of a psychological phenomenon called the contrast effect. This is the tendency of our perception to be influenced by the context or comparison of what we see, hear, feel, or experience. For example, if you touch a cold object and then a warm object, the warm object will feel hotter than if you touched it without touching the cold object first. Similarly, if you see a small object and then a large object, the large object will appear bigger than if you saw it without seeing the small object first.

The contrast effect can be used to influence people's decisions and behaviors in various situations. For instance, if you want to sell a product or service, you can use contrast to make your offer seem more valuable or affordable than the alternatives. You can do this by showing how your product or service is superior to the competitors', or by offering a discount or a bonus that creates a sense of urgency or scarcity. Alternatively, you can use contrast to make your offer seem less risky or costly than the consequences of not taking action. You can do this by highlighting the problems or challenges that your product or service can solve, or by emphasizing the benefits or outcomes that your product or service can deliver.

Another example of using contrast to influence someone is to persuade them to agree with your point of view or opinion. You can do this by presenting two or more arguments or perspectives that are different in some aspect, such as logic, evidence, emotion, credibility, etc. The goal is to make your argument or

58

perspective seem more convincing, compelling, or reasonable than the other(s). You can do this by showing how your argument or perspective is supported by facts, data, examples, testimonials, etc., or by appealing to the values, beliefs, emotions, or interests of your audience. Alternatively, you can use contrast to make your argument or perspective seem less controversial or objectionable than the opposing views. You can do this by acknowledging the validity or merit of the other views, but then showing how they are incomplete, inaccurate, irrelevant, biased, etc.

The model of contrast is a powerful tool for influence because it helps you shape and frame the perception and evaluation of your audience. By using contrast, you can make your offer more attractive or less risky, and your argument more convincing or less controversial. However, you should use contrast ethically and responsibly. Do not use contrast to deceive, manipulate, or exploit your audience. Do not use contrast to create false or exaggerated differences between options or scenarios. Do not use contrast to pressure or coerce your audience into making decisions or taking actions that are against their best interests. Use contrast to inform, educate, and inspire your audience. Use contrast to help them make better choices and achieve better results.

CHAPTER 15: The Process of Negotiation

Negotiation is a form of influence that involves reaching an agreement with another party or parties. Negotiation can be used to resolve conflicts, create value, or achieve goals. Negotiation is not a zero-sum game, where one side wins and the other loses. Rather, negotiation is a collaborative process, where both sides can benefit from finding a mutually acceptable solution.

However, negotiation is not always easy. It requires preparation, communication, and creativity. It also requires an understanding of the interests, needs, and emotions of the other party. In this chapter, we will explore the process of negotiation and how to apply the principles and techniques of influence to achieve win-win outcomes.

The process of negotiation can be divided into four stages: planning, opening, bargaining, and closing. Each stage has its own challenges and opportunities for influence. Let's look at each stage in detail.

Planning

Planning is the stage where you prepare for the negotiation. Planning involves gathering information, setting goals, and developing strategies. Planning is crucial for successful negotiation, as it helps you to:

- Understand the situation and the context of the negotiation
- Identify your own interests, needs, and priorities
- Assess the other party's interests, needs, and priorities
- Anticipate the possible issues and challenges that may arise

60

- Define your best alternative to a negotiated agreement (BATNA)
- Establish your reservation point (the lowest acceptable offer) and your aspiration point (the highest realistic offer)
- Choose the appropriate style and approach for the negotiation

To plan effectively, you need to use the skills of research, analysis, and creativity. You also need to use the principles and techniques of influence to:

- Build rapport and trust with the other party
- Frame the negotiation as a problem-solving opportunity
- Use storytelling to convey your perspective and values
- Use questioning to elicit information and feedback
- Use listening to understand the other party's perspective and emotions
- Use mirroring to demonstrate empathy and alignment
- Use reciprocity to create goodwill and cooperation
- Use scarcity to increase the perceived value of your offer
- Use authority to establish credibility and expertise
- Use social proof to show support and consensus
- Use liking to enhance your attractiveness and likability
- Use commitment and consistency to elicit agreement and action

Opening

Opening is the stage where you initiate the negotiation. Opening involves making contact, setting the agenda, and exchanging information. Opening is important for successful negotiation, as it helps you to:

- Establish a positive tone and atmosphere for the negotiation
- Clarify the purpose and scope of the negotiation
- Share your expectations and preferences for the negotiation process
- Identify common ground and areas of agreement
- Explore differences and areas of disagreement

To open effectively, you need to use the skills of communication, persuasion, and rapport-building. You also need to use the principles and techniques of influence to:

- Use framing to present your offer in a favorable way

61

- Use storytelling to illustrate your points and benefits
- Use questioning to probe for information and interests
- Use listening to acknowledge and validate the other party's points and concerns
- Use mirroring to reinforce rapport and understanding
- Use reciprocity to offer concessions or incentives
- Use scarcity to create urgency or exclusivity
- Use authority to demonstrate confidence and competence
- Use social proof to highlight popularity or demand
- Use liking to express appreciation and compliment
- Use commitment and consistency to seek confirmation and commitment

Bargaining

Bargaining is the stage where you exchange offers, counteroffers, proposals, and concessions. Bargaining involves exploring options, generating alternatives, evaluating outcomes, and reaching agreements. Bargaining is essential for successful negotiation, as it helps you to:

- Create value by expanding the pie or finding win-win solutions
- Claim value by dividing the pie or finding fair distributions
- Resolve conflicts by addressing issues or finding trade-offs
- Achieve goals by meeting interests or satisfying needs

To bargain effectively, you need to use the skills of creativity, problem-solving, and decision-making. You also need to use the principles and techniques of influence to:

- Use framing to emphasize benefits or minimize costs
- Use storytelling to justify your position or persuade your counterpart
- Use questioning to test assumptions or challenge objections
- Use listening to show interest or signal agreement
- Use mirroring to signal flexibility or willingness
- Use reciprocity to exchange concessions or rewards
- Use scarcity to increase leverage or pressure
- Use authority to assert power or influence
- Use social proof to leverage norms or standards
- Use liking to maintain rapport or harmony

62

- Use commitment and consistency to reinforce agreements or actions

Closing

Closing is the stage where you finalize the negotiation. Closing involves summarizing, confirming, documenting, and implementing the agreement. Closing is critical for successful negotiation, as it helps you to:

- Ensure clarity and accuracy of the agreement
- Prevent misunderstandings or disputes
- Build trust and satisfaction
- Foster long-term relationships

To close effectively, you need to use the skills of summarizing, confirming, and documenting. You also need to use the principles and techniques of influence to:

- Use framing to highlight the value and benefits of the agreement
- Use storytelling to celebrate the success and achievements of the negotiation
- Use questioning to clarify any doubts or concerns
- Use listening to acknowledge any feedback or suggestions
- Use mirroring to express gratitude and appreciation
- Use reciprocity to offer support or assistance
- Use scarcity to emphasize the uniqueness or exclusivity of the agreement
- Use authority to endorse or ratify the agreement
- Use social proof to publicize or promote the agreement
- Use liking to compliment or congratulate the other party
- Use commitment and consistency to follow through or deliver on the agreement

Conclusion

Negotiation is a process of influence that can help you achieve your goals and create value for yourself and others. Negotiation is not a one-time event, but a continuous and dynamic process that requires planning, opening, bargaining, and closing. By applying the principles and techniques of influence, you can enhance your negotiation skills and become a master influencer.

CHAPTER 16: The Challenge of Resistance

You have learned the principles, techniques and strategies of influence. You have practiced the skills of storytelling, framing, questioning, listening and mirroring. You have applied the tools of reciprocity, scarcity, authority, social proof, liking, commitment and consistency and contrast. You have mastered the process of negotiation. You are ready to persuade, negotiate and inspire others with your influence.

But what if you encounter resistance? What if your audience is not receptive to your message, your offer or your proposal? What if they have objections, doubts or concerns that prevent them from agreeing with you or taking action? How do you overcome resistance and turn it into acceptance?

Resistance is a natural and inevitable part of influence. It is a sign that your audience is engaged and interested in what you have to say. It is also an opportunity for you to demonstrate your value, credibility and trustworthiness. Resistance is not a barrier to influence, but a challenge that can be overcome with the right approach.

In this chapter, you will learn how to handle resistance effectively and respectfully. You will discover how to:

- Identify the sources and types of resistance
- Anticipate and prevent resistance before it arises
- Acknowledge and validate resistance when it occurs
- Address and resolve resistance with logic, emotion and action
- Follow up and follow through after overcoming resistance

64

Identify the sources and types of resistance

One of the challenges that leaders face when trying to influence others is dealing with resistance. Resistance is the opposition or reluctance to change one's behavior, attitude, or opinion in response to an influence attempt. Resistance can come from various sources and take different forms, depending on the situation and the people involved. In this text, we will identify some of the common sources and types of resistance, and discuss how they can affect the influence process.

Sources of resistance

Resistance can originate from different sources, such as:

- **The influencer:** The person who tries to exert influence may be a source of resistance if they lack credibility, trustworthiness, or expertise in the eyes of the target. For example, if a manager tries to persuade their employees to adopt a new work method, but the employees do not respect or trust the manager, they may resist the change.

- **The target:** The person who is being influenced may be a source of resistance if they have personal or psychological factors that make them resistant to change. For example, if an employee is asked to learn a new skill, but they have low self-efficacy or fear of failure, they may resist the learning opportunity.

- **The message:** The content or delivery of the influence attempt may be a source of resistance if it is unclear, inconsistent, or incompatible with the target's values, beliefs, or needs. For example, if a salesperson tries to convince a customer to buy a product, but the product does not match the customer's preferences or expectations, they may resist the purchase.

- **The context:** The situation or environment in which the influence attempt takes place may be a source of resistance if it is unfavorable, uncertain, or threatening to the target. For example, if a teacher tries to motivate their students to study harder, but the students are facing stress, pressure, or distractions from other sources, they may resist the motivation.

Types of resistance

Resistance can manifest in different ways, such as:

- **Passive resistance:** This is when the target does not openly oppose or reject the influence attempt, but does not comply or cooperate either. They may ignore, avoid, delay, or pretend to agree with the influencer, but do not follow through with the desired behavior change. For example, if an employee agrees to attend a training session, but does not show up or pay attention during the session.

- **Active resistance:** This is when the target openly opposes or rejects the influence attempt, and tries to prevent or reverse the behavior change. They may argue, criticize, complain, or sabotage the influencer's efforts. For example, if an employee protests against a new policy, and tries to persuade their colleagues to join them.

- **Compliance:** This is when the target accepts and follows the influence attempt, but does not internalize or endorse it. They may comply out of fear, reward, or obligation, but do not change their attitude or opinion. For example, if an employee adopts a new work method because their manager rewards them for doing so, but they do not believe in its effectiveness.

- **Commitment:** This is when the target accepts and follows the influence attempt, and also internalizes and endorses it. They may commit out of identification, respect, or conviction. They change their behavior as well as their attitude and opinion. For example, if an employee adopts a new work method because they trust their manager and see its benefits.

<u>Implications for influence</u>

Understanding the sources and types of resistance can help leaders to design and implement more effective influence strategies. By identifying and addressing the potential sources of resistance before they arise, leaders can increase their credibility, trustworthiness, and expertise; tailor their message to match their target's values, beliefs, and needs; and create a favorable and supportive context for change. By recognizing and responding to the different types of resistance as they occur, leaders can use appropriate tactics to overcome passive and active resistance; reinforce compliance with positive feedback and rewards; and foster commitment with involvement and empowerment.

By applying these steps, you will be able to turn resistance into acceptance, and acceptance into action. You will be able to influence others with confidence and integrity, and achieve your desired outcomes.

CHAPTER 17: The Ethic of Influence

Influence is a powerful force that can be used for good or evil. It can help you achieve your goals, persuade others to support your cause, and inspire positive change in the world. But it can also be abused, manipulated, and exploited to serve selfish interests, harm others, and undermine trust and credibility.

How can you ensure that you use influence ethically and responsibly? How can you avoid crossing the line between persuasion and manipulation? How can you respect the autonomy, dignity, and rights of those you influence? How can you balance your own needs and interests with those of others? How can you maintain your integrity and reputation as an influencer?

These are some of the questions that this chapter will address. We will explore the ethical principles and guidelines that should inform your practice of influence. We will also discuss the common ethical dilemmas and challenges that influencers face, and how to resolve them. We will also examine the benefits and consequences of ethical and unethical influence, both for yourself and for others.

The Ethical Principles of Influence

Ethics is the study of moral values and principles that guide human conduct. It is concerned with what is right and wrong, good and bad, fair and unfair, in human interactions. Ethics helps us to evaluate our actions and decisions, and to justify them to ourselves and others.

Influence is a form of human interaction that involves changing or affecting the thoughts, feelings, or behaviors of others. Therefore, influence is subject to ethical evaluation as well. As an influencer, you have a moral responsibility to use your

68

influence in a way that is consistent with your values and principles, and that respects the values and principles of others.

But what are the ethical principles of influence? There is no definitive answer to this question, as different ethical theories and perspectives may have different criteria for judging the morality of influence. However, some common ethical principles that are widely accepted and applied in various fields and contexts are:

- **The principle of respect:** This principle requires you to respect the autonomy, dignity, and rights of those you influence. You should not coerce, deceive, or manipulate them into doing something they do not want to do or that goes against their values or interests. You should also respect their privacy, confidentiality, and consent. You should treat them as ends in themselves, not as means to your ends.

- **The principle of beneficence:** This principle requires you to use your influence for good, not for evil. You should aim to promote the well-being, happiness, and welfare of those you influence, not to harm them or cause them suffering. You should also consider the impact of your influence on society and the environment, and seek to contribute to the common good.

- **The principle of justice:** This principle requires you to use your influence fairly and equitably. You should not discriminate, favor, or prejudice anyone based on irrelevant factors such as race, gender, age, religion, or status. You should also not exploit or take advantage of anyone's vulnerability or ignorance. You should give everyone an equal opportunity to express their views and preferences, and to participate in the decision-making process.

- **The principle of honesty:** This principle requires you to use your influence truthfully and transparently. You should not lie, mislead, or exaggerate about yourself, your products, your services, or your intentions. You should also not omit or conceal any relevant information that may affect the judgment or choice of those you influence. You should disclose any conflicts of interest or potential biases that may affect your credibility or objectivity.

- **The principle of responsibility:** This principle requires you to use your influence accountably and reliably. You should not abuse or misuse your power or authority over others. You should also not shirk or evade your

69

duties or obligations as an influencer. You should follow through on your promises and commitments, and deliver on your expectations. You should also acknowledge and correct any mistakes or errors that may occur as a result of your influence.

These are some of the ethical principles that can help you use your influence in a moral way. They are not absolute rules that apply in every situation, but rather general guidelines that need to be interpreted and applied according to the specific circumstances and context. They are also not mutually exclusive or exhaustive, but rather complementary and overlapping. They may sometimes conflict or compete with each other, requiring you to balance or prioritize them based on the situation.

The Ethical Dilemmas of Influence

Influence is the ability to affect the behavior, opinions, or decisions of others. It is a powerful tool that can be used for good or evil, depending on the intentions and methods of the influencer. Influence can be exerted through various channels, such as persuasion, manipulation, coercion, deception, or inspiration. Each of these channels has its own ethical implications and challenges, which require careful consideration and evaluation by the influencer and the influenced.

Persuasion is the process of convincing someone to adopt a certain belief, attitude, or action through rational arguments, evidence, or appeals to emotions. Persuasion is generally considered to be a positive and ethical form of influence, as it respects the autonomy and dignity of the influenced. However, persuasion can also be unethical if it involves lying, exaggerating, omitting, or distorting relevant information, or if it exploits the vulnerabilities, biases, or emotions of the influenced. Persuasion can also be harmful if it leads to undesirable or harmful outcomes for the influenced or others.

Manipulation is the process of influencing someone to act in a certain way by using subtle, indirect, or deceptive means. Manipulation differs from persuasion in that it does not appeal to the reason or emotions of the influenced, but rather to their subconscious motives, desires, or fears. Manipulation is generally considered to be a negative and unethical form of influence, as it violates the autonomy and dignity of the influenced. However, manipulation can also be ethical if it is used for benevolent purposes, such as helping someone overcome an addiction, phobia, or mental disorder. Manipulation can also be beneficial if it leads to desirable or beneficial outcomes for the influenced or others.

70

Coercion is the process of influencing someone to act in a certain way by using force, threats, or intimidation. Coercion differs from persuasion and manipulation in that it does not rely on any form of communication or interaction with the influenced, but rather on physical or psychological pressure. Coercion is generally considered to be a negative and unethical form of influence, as it violates the autonomy and dignity of the influenced. However, coercion can also be ethical if it is used for legitimate purposes, such as enforcing laws, maintaining order, or protecting rights. Coercion can also be necessary if it prevents harm or injustice for the influenced or others.

Deception is the process of influencing someone to act in a certain way by concealing or misrepresenting the truth. Deception differs from persuasion and manipulation in that it does not involve any form of argumentation or appeal with the influenced, but rather on creating false impressions or beliefs. Deception is generally considered to be a negative and unethical form of influence, as it violates the trust and honesty between the influencer and the influenced. However, deception can also be ethical if it is used for noble purposes, such as saving lives, preventing wars, or promoting peace. Deception can also be justified if it protects privacy or confidentiality for the influencer or others.

Inspiration is the process of influencing someone to act in a certain way by arousing their enthusiasm, creativity, or passion. Inspiration differs from persuasion and manipulation in that it does not involve any form of logic or emotion with the influenced, but rather on stimulating their imagination or spirit. Inspiration is generally considered to be a positive and ethical form of influence, as it enhances the potential and well-being of the influenced. However, inspiration can also be unethical if it involves idolizing, flattering, or exploiting the influencer, or if it induces fanaticism, irrationality, or extremism in the influenced. Inspiration can also be dangerous if it leads to unrealistic or harmful expectations or actions for the influencer or others.

In conclusion, influence is a complex and multifaceted phenomenon that poses various ethical dilemmas for both the influencer and the influenced. Influence can be used for good or evil, depending on the intentions and methods of the influencer. Influence can also have positive or negative consequences, depending on the outcomes and impacts of the influenced.

Therefore, influence requires careful consideration and evaluation by both parties, as well as respect, responsibility, and accountability.

CHAPTER 18: The Practice of Influence

You have learned the theory and the principles of influence. You have explored the tools and techniques that can help you persuade, negotiate and inspire others. You have understood the psychology and the ethics of influence. But how do you put it all into practice? How do you apply what you have learned to your everyday life and work? How do you become a master influencer?

Let's now share some practical tips and strategies that will help you hone your skills and improve your results. We will also give you some exercises and challenges that will test your abilities and push you to the next level. Whether you want to influence your boss, your colleagues, your clients, your friends or your family, these suggestions will help you achieve your goals and make a positive impact.

Tip #1: Know your purpose

Before you attempt to influence anyone, you need to have a clear idea of what you want to achieve and why. What is your desired outcome? What is your motivation? What are the benefits for you and for others? Having a clear purpose will help you focus your efforts, communicate your message and measure your progress. It will also help you align your actions with your values and avoid unethical or manipulative tactics.

Tip #2: Know your audience

The next step is to understand who you are trying to influence and what makes them tick. What are their needs, wants, interests, preferences, goals, fears, challenges, beliefs, values and emotions? How do they perceive you and the situation? What are their expectations and objections? How do they prefer to

72

communicate and receive information? The more you know about your audience, the more you can tailor your approach and appeal to their motivations.

Tip #3: Know yourself

Influence is not only about others, but also about yourself. You need to be aware of your own strengths, weaknesses, biases, emotions and tendencies. How do you react under pressure or in conflict? How do you cope with uncertainty or ambiguity? How do you deal with feedback or criticism? How do you handle success or failure? How do you learn from your mistakes or improve your skills? Being self-aware will help you manage yourself effectively, adapt to different situations and grow as an influencer.

Tip #4: Plan ahead

Influence is not something that happens by chance or by luck. It requires preparation and strategy. Before you engage in any influence attempt, you need to plan ahead and anticipate the possible scenarios. What are the best ways to approach your audience and deliver your message? What are the potential obstacles or risks that might arise? How will you overcome them or mitigate them? What are the alternatives or backup plans if things don't go as expected? Planning ahead will help you be prepared, confident and flexible.

Tip #5: Practice regularly

Influence is a skill that can be learned and improved with practice. The more you practice, the more comfortable and proficient you will become. You can practice in different ways: by observing others who are good at influencing; by asking for feedback from people who know you well; by reading books or articles on influence; by taking courses or workshops on influence; by joining clubs or groups that focus on influence; by finding mentors or coaches who can guide you; by setting yourself goals or challenges that require influence; by applying what you have learned to real-life situations. Practicing regularly will help you develop your habits, refine your techniques and enhance your results.

73

CHAPTER 19: The Future of Influence

Influence is not a static skill that remains the same over time. It is a dynamic and evolving art that adapts to the changing needs, preferences and expectations of the people we want to persuade, negotiate and inspire. In this chapter, we will explore some of the trends and challenges that will shape the future of influence in the coming years.

One of the most significant trends is the rise of digital and social media, which have transformed the way we communicate, interact and influence others. Digital and social media offer new opportunities and platforms for influencing, such as blogs, podcasts, videos, webinars, online courses, e-books, social networks, online communities, forums, reviews, ratings and more. These media allow us to reach a wider and more diverse audience, to share our message and expertise, to establish our credibility and authority, to build trust and rapport, to create engagement and loyalty, to generate feedback and referrals, and to measure and optimize our impact.

However, digital and social media also pose new challenges and risks for influencing. For example, we need to be aware of the ethical and legal implications of our online actions, such as respecting privacy, intellectual property and data protection laws. We also need to be mindful of the potential negative effects of our online presence, such as cyberbullying, trolling, fake news, misinformation, disinformation and manipulation. We need to be able to distinguish between credible and unreliable sources of information, to verify facts and evidence, to avoid cognitive biases and logical fallacies, and to resist persuasion attempts that are based on deception or coercion.

Another important trend is the increasing diversity and complexity of the people we want to influence. As the world becomes more globalized, interconnected and

74

multicultural, we encounter people from different backgrounds, cultures, values, beliefs, opinions, preferences and styles. This diversity enriches our perspectives and opportunities, but also challenges our assumptions and stereotypes. We need to be able to adapt our influencing strategies and tactics to the specific context and situation of each person or group we want to influence. We need to be able to understand their needs, motivations, emotions, expectations and goals. We need to be able to communicate effectively across linguistic and cultural barriers. We need to be able to respect their differences and find common ground.

A third major trend is the growing importance of emotional intelligence for influencing. Emotional intelligence is the ability to recognize, understand and manage our own emotions and those of others. It is essential for building trust, rapport and empathy with the people we want to influence. It is also crucial for managing conflict, stress and resistance that may arise during the influencing process. Emotional intelligence helps us to be more self-aware, self-regulated, motivated, empathetic and socially skilled. It enables us to communicate more effectively, persuasively and authentically. It allows us to create positive emotional states in ourselves and others that facilitate influencing.

The future of influence is exciting and challenging. It requires us to constantly learn new skills, tools and techniques that can help us achieve our goals. It also requires us to be ethical, responsible and respectful in our influencing endeavors. Influence is not a one-way street; it is a two-way dialogue that involves listening as much as speaking; understanding as much as explaining; collaborating as much as competing; inspiring as much as persuading.

75

CHAPTER 20: The Mastery of Influence

Influence is not a skill that you can learn overnight. It takes years of practice, observation, and refinement to master the art of influencing others. Influence is not about manipulation or coercion, but about understanding human psychology, emotions, and motivations. Influence is not about getting what you want, but about creating win-win situations for everyone involved. Influence is not about being selfish or arrogant, but about being humble and respectful.

Reciprocity, commitment and consistency, social proof, liking, authority, and scarcity are some of the principles of persuasion that can influence people's behavior and decisions. Let's look at each one in more detail with some examples.

- Reciprocity means that people tend to return favors and feel obligated to those who have helped them or given them something valuable. For example, if a friend invites you to their birthday party, you may feel obliged to invite them to yours. Or if a salesperson gives you a free sample, you may feel more inclined to buy something from them.

- Commitment and consistency means that people tend to stick to their decisions and actions, especially if they have made them publicly or voluntarily. For example, if you sign a petition for a cause, you may be more likely to donate money or volunteer for it later. Or if you tell your friends that you are going to quit smoking, you may be more motivated to follow through.

- Social proof means that people tend to follow the behavior and opinions of others, especially if they are similar to them or have authority or expertise. For example, if you see a lot of positive reviews for a product,

76

you may be more persuaded to buy it. Or if you see a celebrity endorsing a brand, you may be more influenced by their opinion.

- Liking means that people tend to be more influenced by those who they like, trust, or admire. For example, if you have a good rapport with your boss, you may be more willing to accept their suggestions. Or if you find someone attractive, you may be more receptive to their requests.

- Authority means that people tend to obey or respect those who have power, status, or credibility. For example, if a doctor tells you to take a medication, you may be more likely to follow their advice. Or if a police officer tells you to stop at a red light, you may be more likely to comply.

- Scarcity means that people tend to value more what is rare, limited, or exclusive. For example, if a product is on sale for a limited time, you may be more tempted to buy it. Or if a club has a long waiting list, you may be more eager to join it.

- These are some of the ways that persuasion can work on us. By understanding these principles, we can become more aware of how we are influenced by others and how we can influence others ourselves.

The main techniques of influence are:

- **Framing:** How you present your message or offer can affect how people perceive it and respond to it. You can use positive or negative framing, contrast effect, anchoring, or storytelling to make your message more appealing or persuasive.

- **Questioning:** Asking the right questions can help you uncover the needs, goals, values, and preferences of your audience. You can use open-ended or closed-ended questions, probing questions, rhetorical questions, or hypothetical questions to elicit information or feedback.

- **Listening:** Listening actively and empathically can help you build rapport, trust, and understanding with your audience. You can use paraphrasing, reflecting, summarizing, or clarifying to show that you are listening and interested in what they have to say.

77

- **Mirroring**: Mirroring the body language, tone of voice, or words of your audience can help you create rapport, harmony, and alignment with them. You can use matching, pacing, or leading techniques to mirror them subtly and naturally.

- **Persuasion**: Persuasion is the process of changing someone's attitude, belief, or behavior in a desired direction. You can use logic, emotion, or credibility appeals to persuade your audience. You can also use the six principles of influence as persuasion tools.

- **Negotiation**: Negotiation is the process of reaching an agreement that satisfies both parties. You can use preparation, communication, collaboration, compromise, or concession strategies to negotiate effectively. You can also use the BATNA (best alternative to a negotiated agreement) concept to evaluate your options and leverage.

- **Inspiration**: Inspiration is the process of motivating someone to take action or achieve a goal. You can use vision, values, passion, or purpose statements to inspire your audience. You can also use stories, metaphors, analogies, or quotes to illustrate your points and make them memorable.

To apply these principles and techniques in different contexts and scenarios, you need to consider the following factors:

- Your goal: What do you want to achieve? What is your desired outcome?
- Your audience: Who are you trying to influence? What are their needs, goals, values, and preferences? How do they perceive you and your message?
- Your message: What do you want to say? How do you want to say it? What evidence or support do you have for your message?
- Your medium: How will you deliver your message? What channel or format will you use? How will it affect your message and its impact?
- Your timing: When will you deliver your message? What is the best time to influence your audience? How will it affect their attention and receptivity?

To keep improving your influence skills and avoid common pitfalls and mistakes, you need to:

- Practice regularly: The more you practice influencing others in different situations and settings, the more confident and proficient you will become. Seek feedback from others and learn from your successes and failures.

- **Adapt constantly:** The world is changing rapidly and so are people's needs, expectations, and preferences. You need to be flexible and adaptable to different circumstances and challenges. Monitor the results of your influence efforts and adjust accordingly.

- **Learn continuously:** There is always something new to learn about influence and human behavior. You need to be curious and open-minded to new ideas and perspectives. Read books, articles, blogs, podcasts, or videos on influence and related topics. Attend workshops, seminars, courses, or webinars on influence skills.

- **Respect always:** Influence is not a one-way street. You need to respect your audience and their opinions, feelings, and choices. You need to be honest, ethical, and transparent in your influence attempts. You need to avoid manipulation, deception, or coercion. You need to create value for both parties and seek mutual benefit.

Influence is a powerful and valuable skill that can help you achieve your personal and professional goals. It can also help you make a positive difference in the lives of others. By mastering the art of influence, you can persuade, negotiate, and inspire others with confidence and ease.

CONCLUSION: How to Become a Master Influencer

You have reached the end of this book, but not the end of your journey as an influencer. In fact, you have just begun. You have learned the theory and the practice of influence, but you still need to apply them in your own context and situation. You have acquired the tools and techniques of influence, but you still need to sharpen them and use them wisely. You have discovered the principles and the psychology of influence, but you still need to respect them and follow them ethically.

Influence is not a one-time event, but a continuous process. It is not a fixed skill, but a dynamic art. It is not a static trait, but a flexible mindset. Influence is not something you have, but something you do. And to do it well, you need to keep learning, experimenting, adapting and improving.

The best way to become a master influencer is to practice influence every day, in every situation, with every person you encounter. Whether you are persuading your boss, negotiating with your client, inspiring your team, or simply communicating with your family and friends, you can always apply the principles and techniques of influence that you have learned in this book.

But remember, influence is not only about getting what you want, but also about giving what others need. Influence is not only about achieving your goals, but also about helping others achieve theirs. Influence is not only about making an impact, but also about making a difference. Influence is not only about being successful, but also about being significant.

80

So use your influence for good, not for evil. Use your influence to serve, not to manipulate. Use your influence to create value, not to exploit. Use your influence to build trust, not to break it. Use your influence to empower, not to dominate. Use your influence to make the world a better place, not a worse one.

You have the potential to be a master influencer. You have the power to change yourself and others. You have the opportunity to make a positive difference in your life and in the lives of those around you. All you need is the willingness to learn and the courage to act.

So go ahead and unleash your influence. The world is waiting for you.